100 Architectures

Coloring Book

100 Pages of Famous Monuments, European Buildings, Castles, City & Street Designs, Creative Relaxation for Adults

Rachel Mintz

*The book has 105 images. If you see similar ones, they are EXTRA variations we thought you would like.

Join Rachel Mintz Printable Books Club
Free coloring pages, discount coupons, giveaways and more...
It is free to join - Scan below:

Colors Testing Page

This Book
Belongs to:

_____

_____

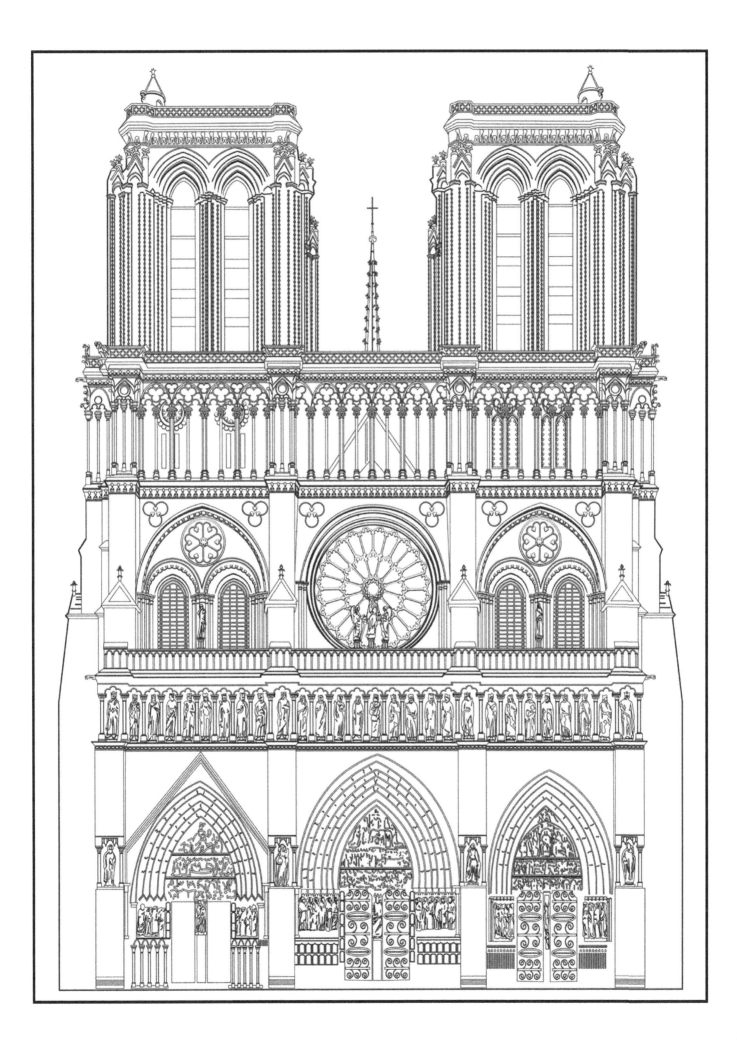

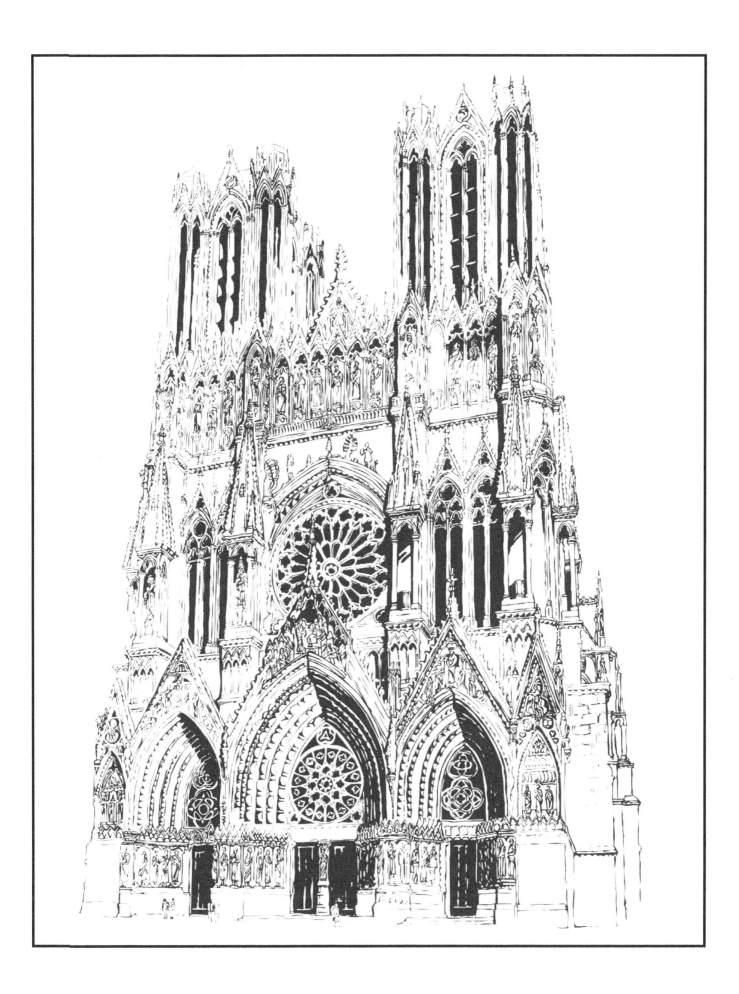

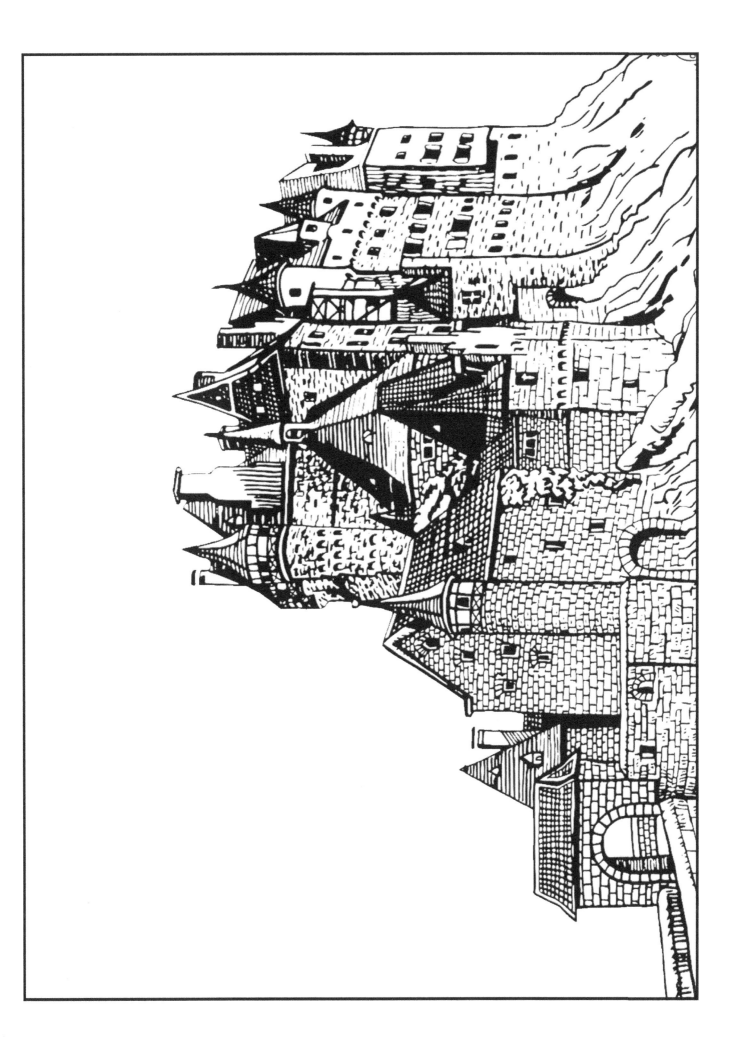

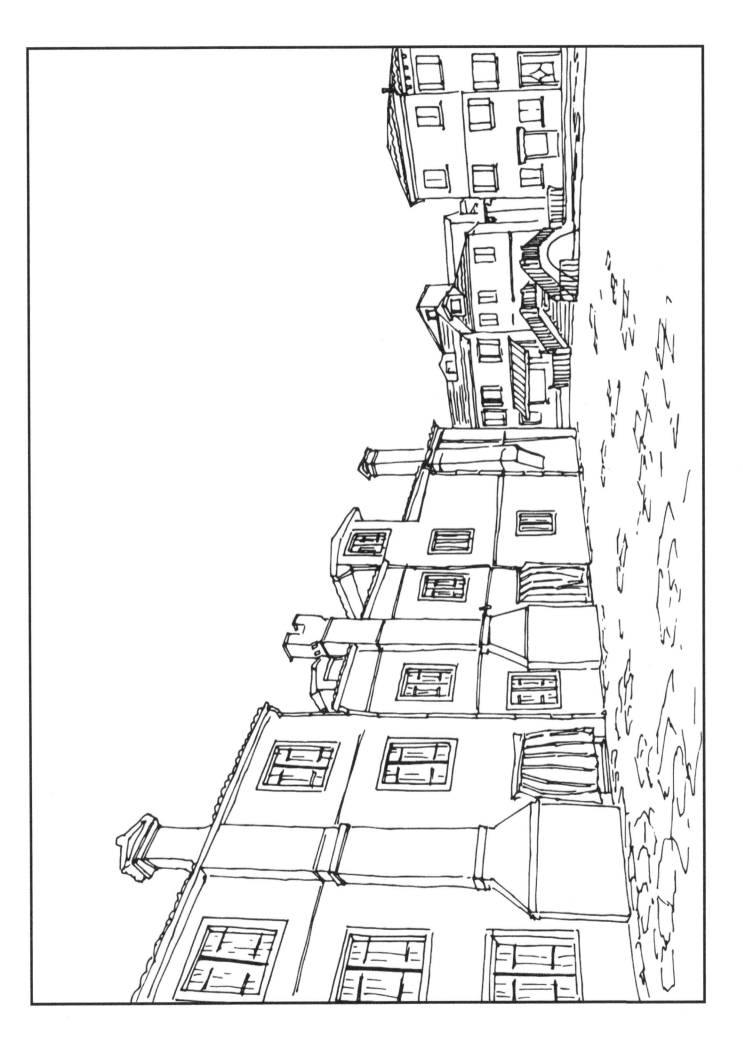

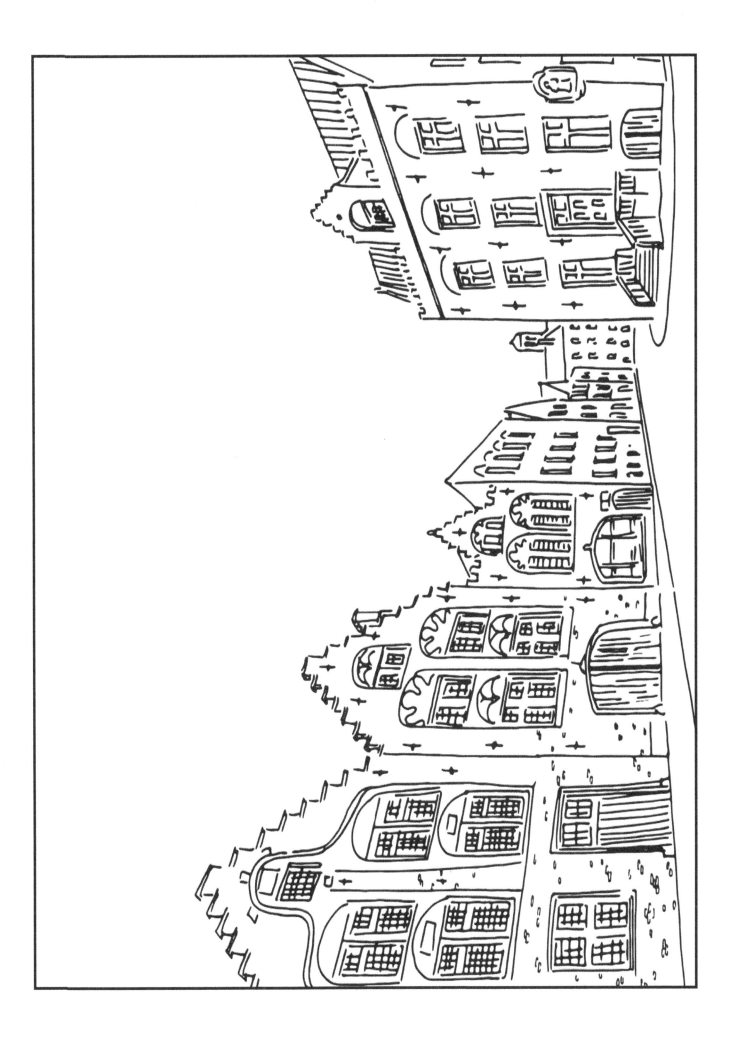

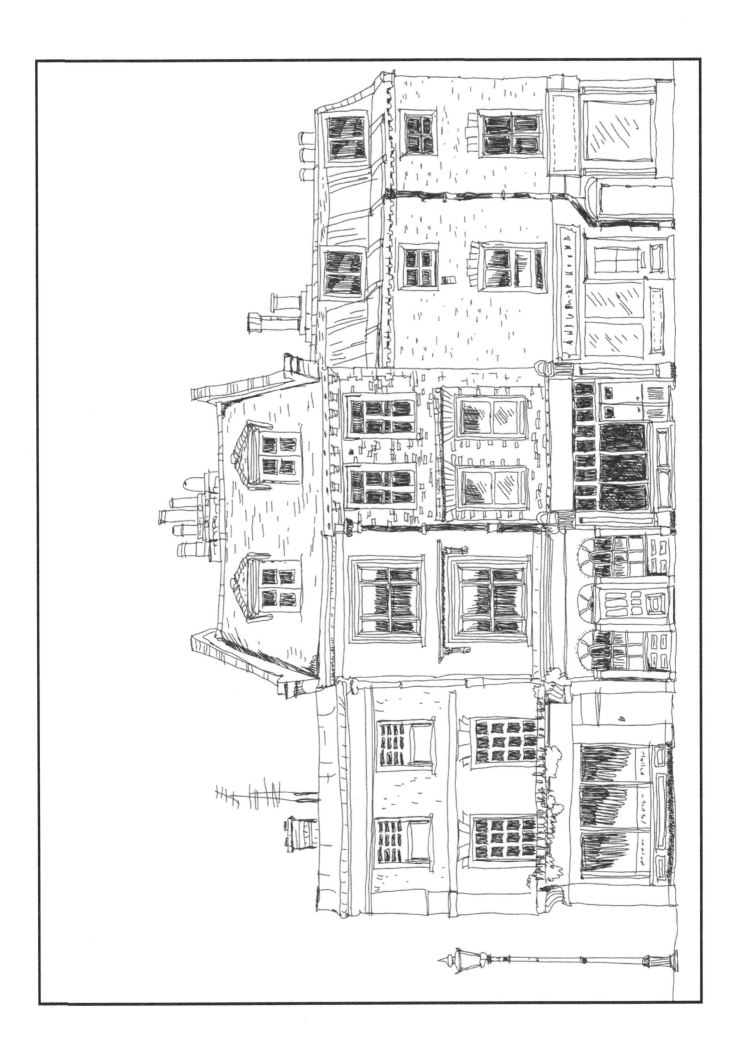

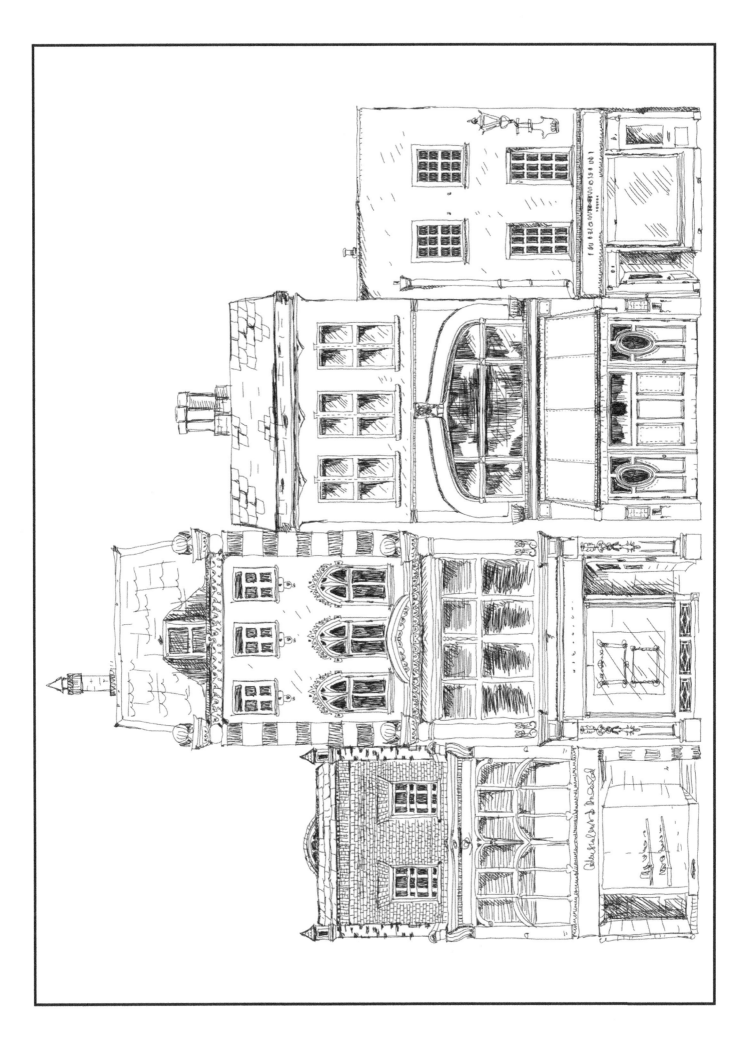

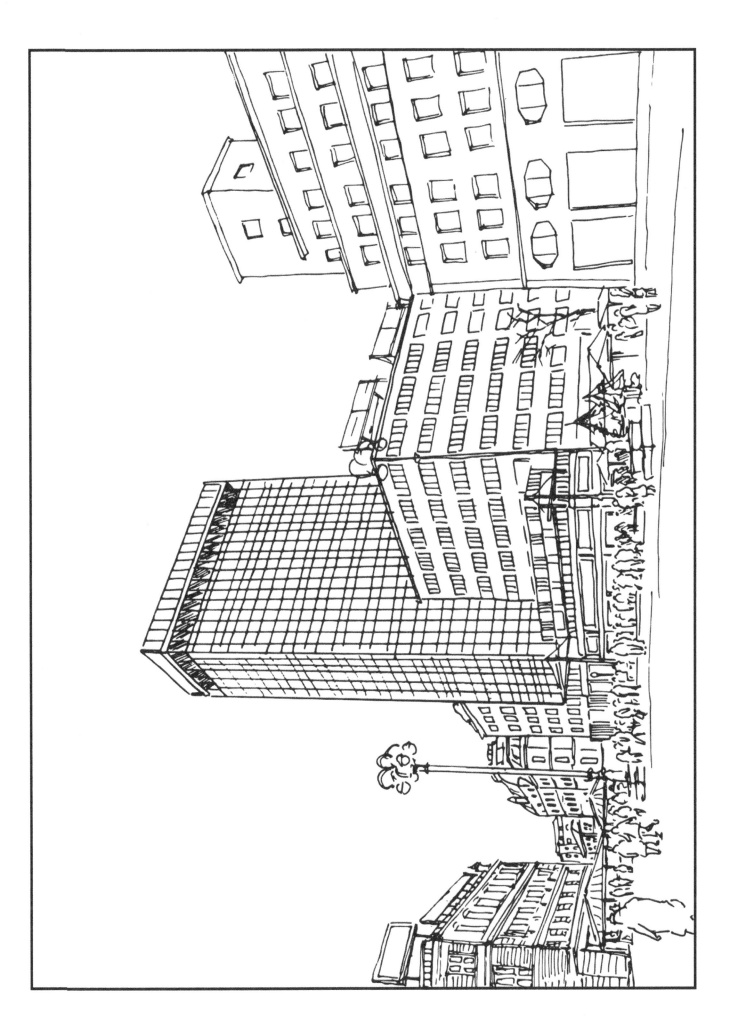

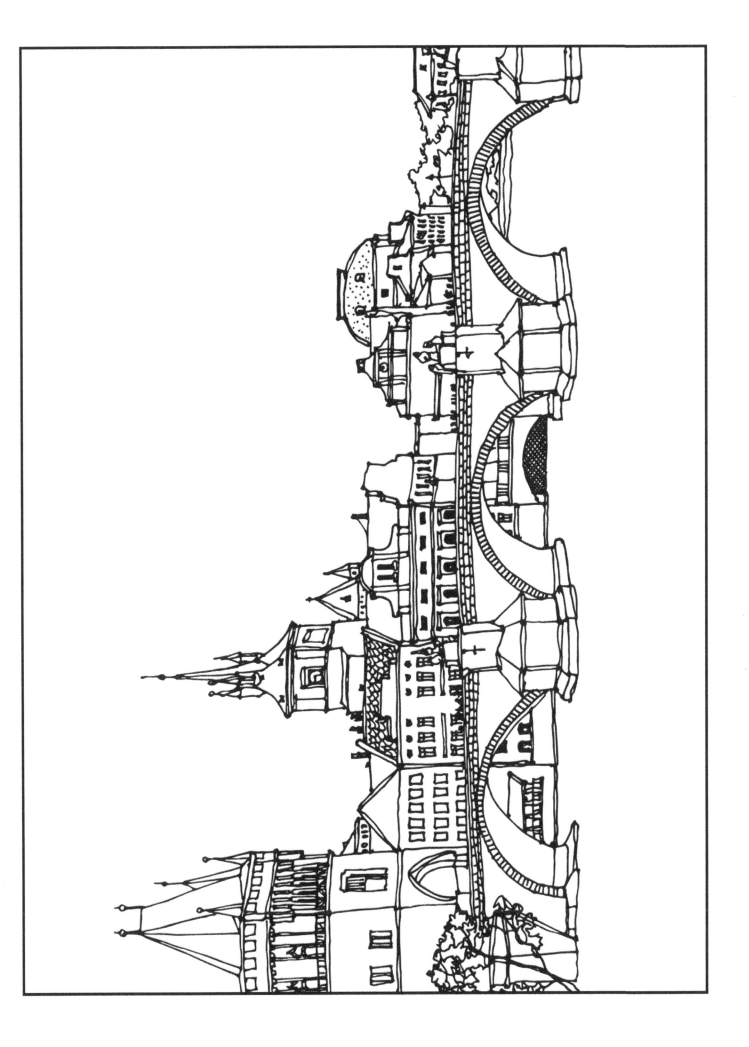

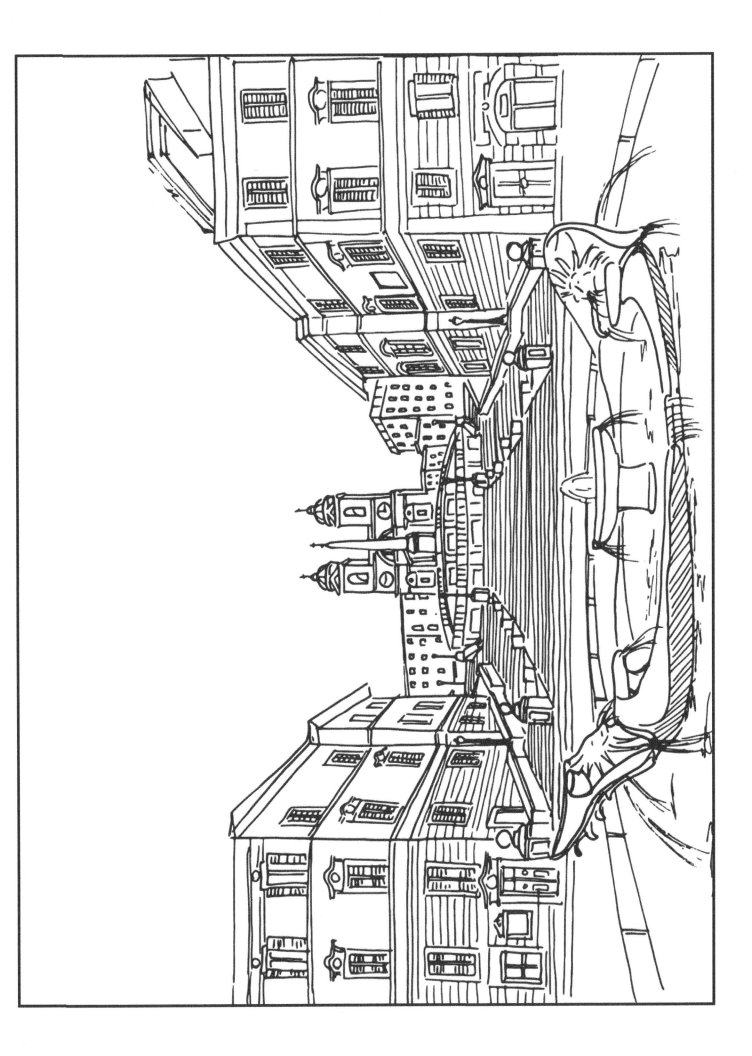

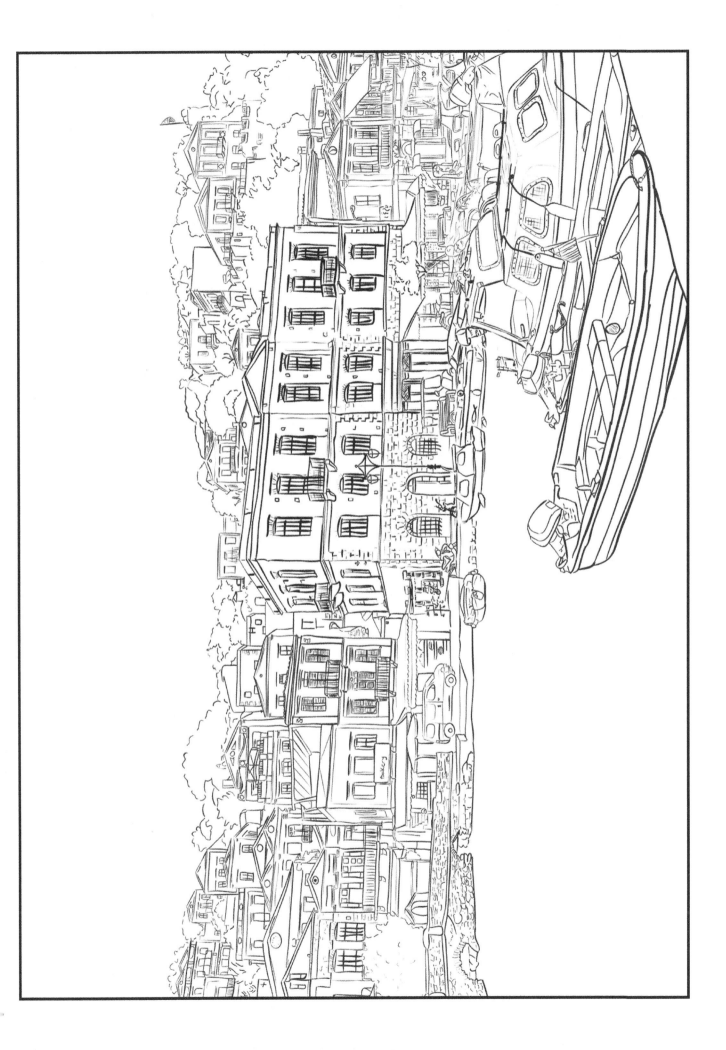

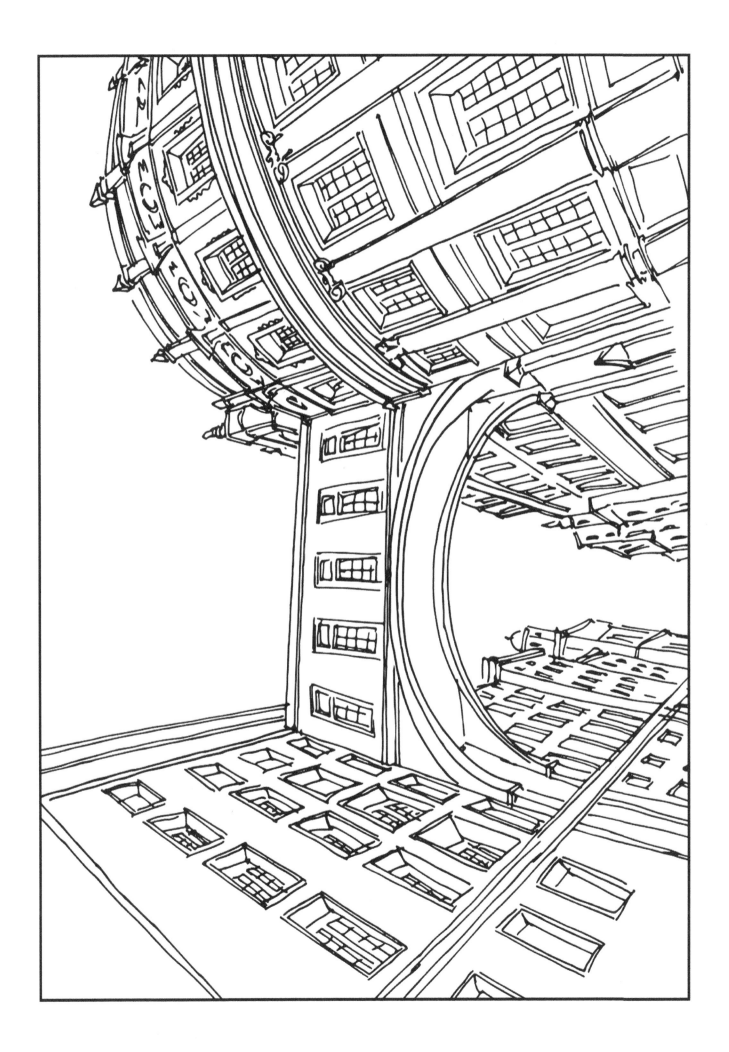

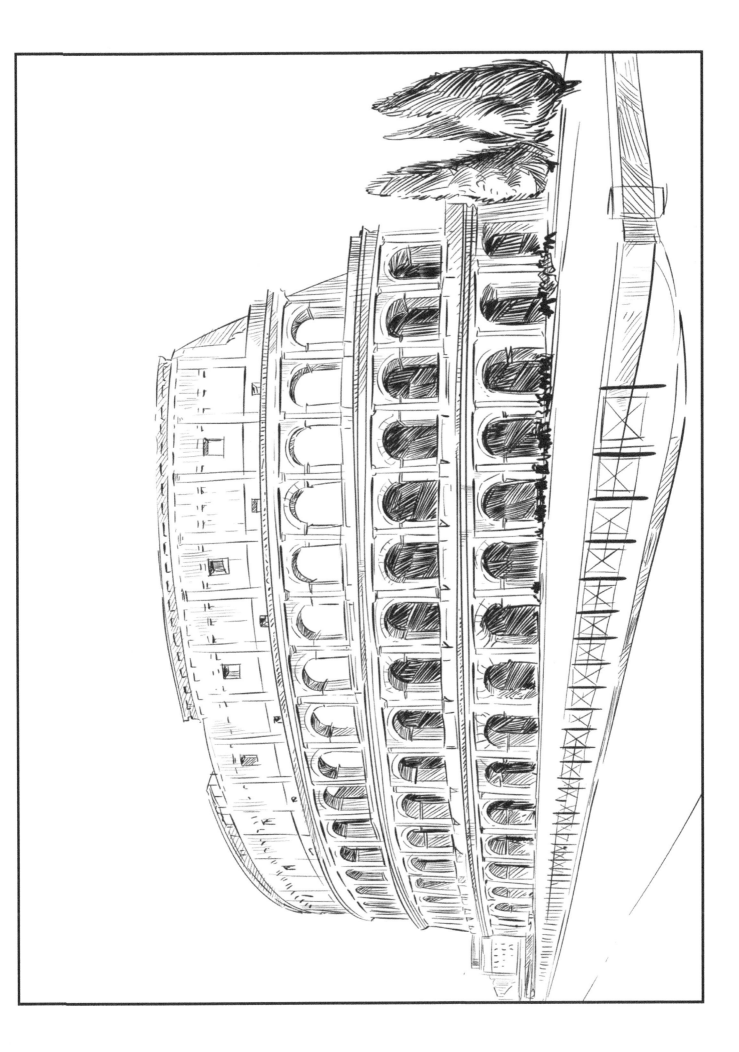

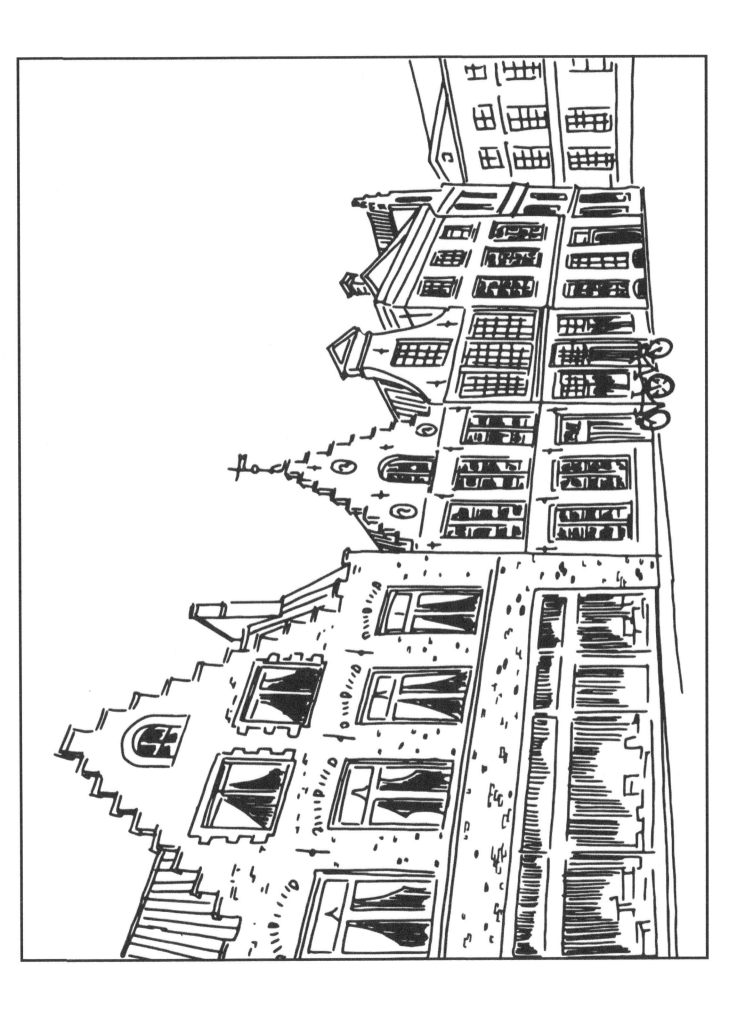

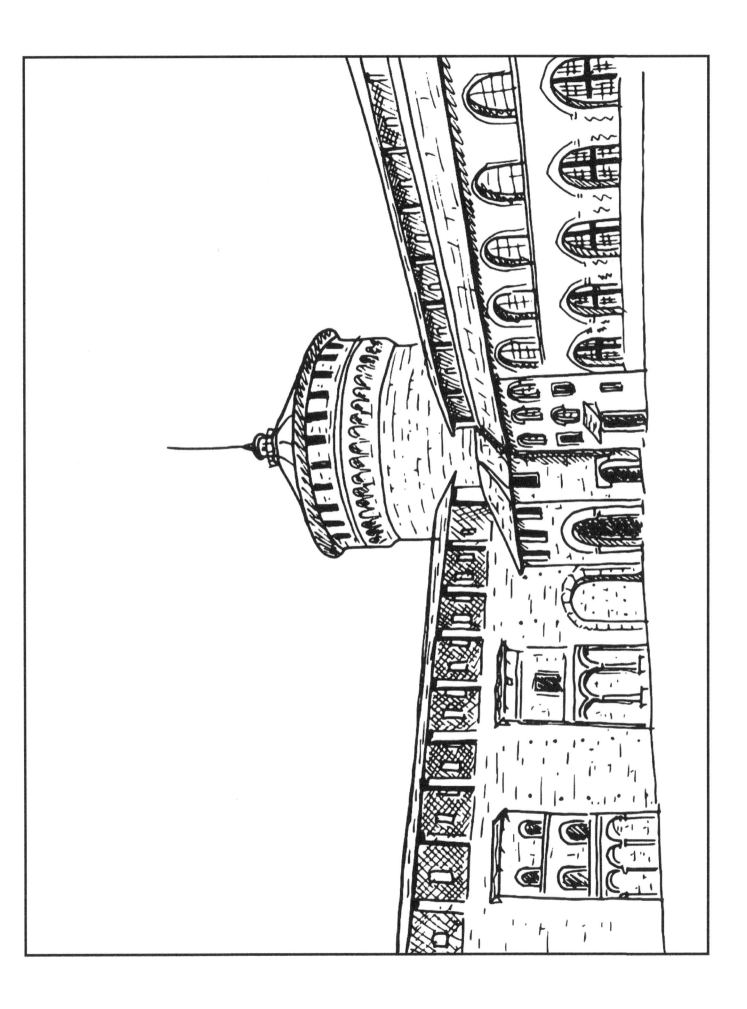

Thank you for coloring with us
We hope you had a wonderful time.

For more **Rachel Mintz** coloring
books to order (Amazon or digital
PDF format books), scan with your
phone the QR codes on the next
pages.

Scan to buy from Amazon:

Scan to download the PDF book:

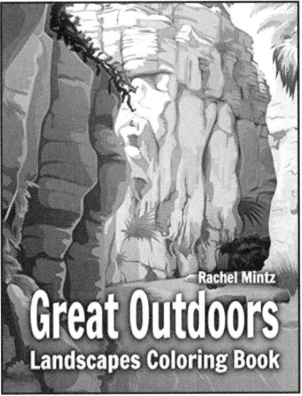

Scan to buy from Amazon:

Scan to download the PDF book:

BEAUTIFUL LIGHTHOUSES
COLORING BOOK

RACHEL MINTZ

Scan to buy from Amazon:

Scan to download the PDF book:

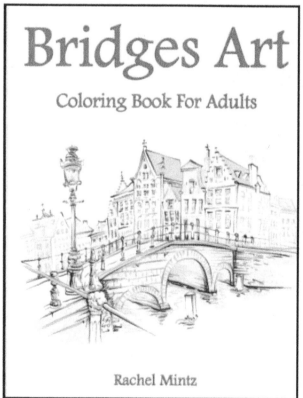

Bridges Art

Coloring Book For Adults

Rachel Mintz

Scan to buy from Amazon:

Scan to download the PDF book:

Scan to buy from Amazon:

Scan to download the PDF book:

Scan to buy from Amazon:

Scan to download the PDF book:

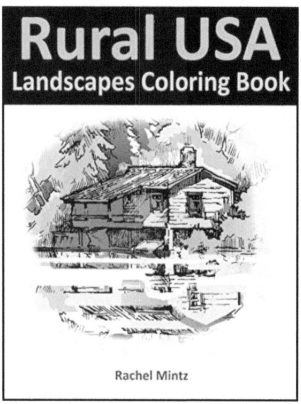

Thank you for coloring with us.

We will be very thankful if you could
rate & **review** on Amazon for this book.

Add your colored pages to the review and show us
and everyone which pages you liked most.